Top 10 ways Drop Outs Become Billionaires

Genius Mehra
Bhoomi

Contents

One Important Story

You have just started reading the book or may be you are not having your copy even. But I want to tell you one of the stories here which is given in the book. This is very important to tell you how to be successful. This is very important if you want to launch a startup, business or do anything new in your family. It is because for that we ask our family for advice and different stuff. So here I want to tell you a few things that are important and you should know even if you don't buy the book. So here is the extract from the book:

Have you also tried doing something different like a start up? Well, most of the people say no to this question because they could never gather this much courage to invest some money on their ideas. And if they invest a little money and they face loss, they leave it. They don't give a second attempt. They themselves don't believe in their ideas. They ask for opinion to people. If they say yes, then they may try but if they deny they start doing doubt on their ideas. But do you know in either case, whether the public advises you to do it or not, you have a loss. Do you know why? Suppose you have any idea.

Lets assume that Google is not created, or any other search engine and you are in 1990's. You got the concept of Google. You asked for advice. What could be the advice of people? Will they say yes, you should do? They will never say yes. In 1990's, people used internet less. So if you would try this search engine start up, it will be a loss to you according to your family and friends. Why, because if it was profitable anyone else would have tried it. Internet was so slow so how could you make good money with it. Advertisers at that time were not investing too much money in online marketing at that time. People didn't have proper knowledge of computers and internet. So did you see that even the idea of Google would have been denied by your family and friends, so just leave any other small idea. But there is one kind of loss left. What if they said yes? Suppose after 5 to 6 years after the introduction of Google you asked your family, then they may say yes, because Google was earning good money. Advertisers were also investing money online. So your family may think that you may also earn good money. But was that really a good option.

Actually, there are tens of search engines but you just don't know them. The reason is that Google has become so popular. So you may have got a loss here also if you applied the same concept of Google. So do you see the effect of a few years. Suppose you had the idea of creating such a search engine and you had resources also. But you didn't want to drop out of college because you are topper in college. You would launch the search engine after graduation. So do you understand what can this time cost you. Sometimes, playing safe is the most dangerous step. You need to take risks, but calculated risks. Suppose if you had launched the search engine before Google and failed in that fight against Google. So are you going to die of hunger? Definitely, no, because if you competed good Google may have seen your capability and farsightedness, get a job there. It is because they may have seen you do original work and you similar thoughts about world future like them. So is getting a job there small for you? Being true, there is no loss for you if you did it.

About This Book

I am a child, very young,

Always speaks of success, my tongue

I just want name, fame,

You may ask my heart or brain.

But now I'm growing, world showing world,

And I understand success isn't like sweetened curd,

I can't succeed, because none can fly like a bird,

Unless they have powerful source, of man not knowing honesty as word.

Now I'm aged, ready to go

The only regret I have, is not trying to row,

They said, path to success was bad,

But mine was also mad,

The other path at least had a way,

And now I need to pay.

World told holes in the dark deeper,

But now, to my regret, they are much lighter,

Before going I tell you, no one told,

Go read the book, before you become me and old.

The poem shows how in childhood we all want success but later get distracted by the world. This book is written to discover one of the very important questions which arises in the minds of everyone that why should we study if drop outs are billionaires. There is no limit to take such successful names and you would be knowing them yourself. So if this is really true then why do we go to schools? Believe me, I will not only talk high of schools. I accept, we should give less time to stupid orthodox study. I used the word orthodox because we even don't know why we are studying, we are just following others, and they are also following others, and finally they are following us as others.

This whole thing is being done for a very long time, I know. I know what it feels like questioning the schools and education. They come up with many counter questions and arguments, which as a child you may not be able to answer but you know it is wrong. The most repeated argument is that whatever you learn will someday be used by you so why don't you want to learn. Well, this thing is totally correct. There is nothing wrong in it and we can never deny it. But you are also not wrong when you question. So, what is this happening that two guys are speaking opposite things and they both are correct? Well, the thing is time. But don't you think that in schools we give more time and energy to what we use less in life. When we question education, we don't want to just stop taking it, but rather we mean, also if you didn't think this before, that it is taking a lot of time which we could give to valuable skills. We want to learn new and future creating skills. We don't want to stop schooling but learn something useful, and if that's not useful then give it minium time. We are ready to learn what they teach in schools but not want to give much time. So, school thinks we want to stop it but rather we just want to give it minimum time and eforts and also don't want to stress from it. When we don't do what we are required, but do what we are passionate about, then we become billionaires.

But, there are many other reasons also that these entrepreneurs became successful, dropping out was not all. What they did was not luck but it could be repeated by young children, and also adults, if they follow a few ways which were followed by them knowing or unknowingly. I do accept that they may have unknowingly done it, being influenced by anyone or anything, but they have done it right to reach these heights. But coincidence does not happen with everyone so everyone can't be here, even after dropping out. But after reading this book you may be able to do this if you are a kid, and if you are an adult then you will get a good direction for your future which will make you very successful. I can't give 100% guarantee of you becoming billionaire but your success is confirmed after reading this book. But remember reading this book is just the pre step of success. Later, you need to take other steps also. If you are really passionate for your success then take steps. Your first step is to buy this book. It is not very expensive but buying this is really a boundary breaking step because then to save the money you have invested, you would need to read the whole book and then you need to work hard and be successful. Believe me it's not very easy, but also not very difficult also. You are not going to get many jokes here, or some gossips, but you are going to get some good advice, amazing short stories of great successful dropt outs as examples, and some very hard working tips, as you would need to follow them. If you think that I am scaring you then sorry, but it is true. I know everyone can't be successful so everyone can't buy this book. But I have expectations with you. Then after this step, you need to read this whole book. You need to read everything and do all the things. So before anything, you need to do two things, buy this book and then read this book. 99% people have now aborted the task of getting success. But after this book, you would not ask anyone what to do in future. You can even guide others about their path to success. May be you become as much successful as your inspiration and your idols may become your rivals. If you do have an idol then please tell me in the review section. But now lets go to the real book. I hope you are in the 1% , or less, reading this book. Well, after certain parts of the book, some question will arise in your mind and I have answered some question in the book. A few question are: Did they get early success in their life? The answer is No, how is explained in the book. How not having a degree helped them? Should we go to School or College? If yes, then till which level? Is the level same for everyone? So I hope that after reading this book these questions will arise in your mind also. So don't worry I have answered them here.

Advice From Author

I don't believe in working hard. Working hard doesn't bring you success and I can prove it here. Tell me a farmer or an investor of stock market, who does more work? Obviously, the farmer works more but why the investor is more successful. This is because of the kind of work. The work of investor is more intellectual than physical. Now I ask, who works more, a small investor or Warren Buffet? A small investor does intraday trading and changes stocks very frequently, but not Warren Buffet. Well, I know that Warren Buffet sir works a lot but how does he work? He reads a lot. Then he analyses everything, and then takes a single step. Not like a small investor, he does not change his stocks every week, or every month. Actually, he works of trying to see the future. This is the reason he is so successful. So did you see, you just can't work hard to become successful. You need to decide what to do, how to do, and what not to do. So this book is for that only. You may get more results than your work. This book is going to give a few very important things that many people neglect. I worked for analyzing everything, so now you should take profit from it, because it would save you your time. So now without wasting any time lets start this book.

Introduction

This question often arises in the minds of young people and even adults also, if drop outs are billionaires then why should we study? Is there really any use of education if drop outs are changing the world and educated people are just buying groceries and paying the bills? They are making the world as they want and we, even can't watch the T.V channel we want(only applicable if you are a married man), we are just fulfilling orders of our stupid bosses. Why is there so much difference between us and them? Technically, we are more educated than them but being true, if I remove this word, technically, then the condition is reversed. But just leave this for this time and in the book it is clearly explained. If I needed to sum up the whole book in one single point, then the point was that they focused on their power and then they used their power. If I ask you, have you used all your talents and skills which you have, then what will be your answer? I am hundred and one percent sure, your answer is a big no. You definitely have not used all your skills. But now comes the second question, have you tried to gain more skills and knowledge in the past? And in that attempt have you learnt that skill?

I suppose that you may be giving this answer in Yes, but if your answer is no, then we will talk later. So if you answered yes, then sorry to say that your hard work and time have been wasted, because you have not used your knowledge and skill which you gained, so if you don't use something then it is waste. If you would have focused on using the skills you already have and develop them then may be you would have become more successful than you are today. This book consists of many stories taken from some of the most successful people and I hope that you would love this book, and after reading this book you would come to know that why drop outs become billionaires. But remember you only know a handful of successful drop outs, but no one knows drop outs who failed!!!

Do you know the names of a few billionaires who dropped out? Well, I hope that you may be knowing some names of such people because they have made them so big and powerful, that if you don't know them then you are considered to be a stupid. So I hope that you are not a stupid, so you would have given me a few names. So I promise that most of the names would be read by you in this book. I have written their names and case studies because I want to give examples. This is going to be very knowledgeable book for you if you read this with the hunger of knowledge.

So now in this book, I am going to give you points that why the need of education is not over and till which level we should study. But here I want to clarify that they didn't drop out because they wanted but the thing is that they were forced by the work load. Everything will be clarified in this book in detail. We need education but it does not mean to run behind getting good marks and grades. Education is a broad term so it should not be limited to just marks and a few subjects like Maths, Science, Business Studies, and others. Education is also not limited to class, but education means learning from the whole Universe.

From a clock we learn to be always on time, from a fan we learn to work hard to give relief to someone else, from shoes we learn to carry the load of someone else because it is your duty. So learning can be done at any place, and being true, what you learn outside the classroom is real education. It is because you study that not because you are forced to do that but you want to do. You will not get marks for that but you do that because you are interested in doing that. You can even make your passion your profession later in your life. But for that you need to have a passion. I don't want to be harsh, but you can't develop a passion in the classroom. You remain on fast running horse in the classroom because your teacher is teaching you to complete the syllabus, and then you need to learn that, to write in the exams. If you could not understand then you need to cram it, and it is very common nowadays. It is so common because the motive of schooling is to get marks.

Schools want their students to work hard and get marks, parents want their kids to get good marks in the exams. School wants it so that they could show a good result of their students so that they could get new admissions now easily and they could increase the fees of their school. No one would go to an expensive school if the education is not good, and education is measured in terms of marks of students. And parents want their children to get good marks because they want to show off in their family and in their neighbourhood. They also want their children to be secured in their life for which they need a good job, and these marks and a good degree could help them in that. So the children would be having a secure future.

Children are pressurized from everywhere that they want to drop out, but it is not the solution. Many drop outs are billionaires, and majority of billionaires are dropped out of college, but dropping out is not the way to do anything. Education system and attitude of schools and parents is not so good but kids need to be educated up to a certain level. I don't mean up to a degree or qualification level. This level is different for everyone and you will come to know about that deeply in the book. So I think that now the main topics should be started so that you all can come to know what you all want. So now let's start this book here

Chapter 1: They Made Them Highly Skilled

This is obviously a very important skill. Since childhood they have been doing things that others could not even imagine. They tried to develop their skills. They just didn't read books and then believe that they will do it in future. I ask you this question. Has it ever happened that you read something about any skill or anything else, then you said that you will do it in future or you want to learn that skill in future? It may be about new things about the skills which you already have. I am sure you have said yes, for this question. It happens most of the times that people read new things and then they say that in future they will do it. But believe me if you can't do something today then you can't do it tomorrow.

Tomorrow is going to be the same as today. I accept that may be tomorrow conditions for you become easy. But the time when you learn that thing will be more when you start late. I accept time utilized will be more in the first case but the second case is not beneficial. I give you an example: You and your friend want to learn how to play Football. So you both read about it then you supposed that you should play it later on in future, but your friend started playing it. You didn't try it at all, but you just said in future. Then later on, somehow you started.

This rarely happens that you start doing something which you left for future. It is extremely rare but just believe that you did it. Then starting was easy for you. You may soon start doing good dribbling, you can shoot with more power than in your young age, but. You may be remembering about the friend I referred. You can play it well, but can you think of competing with your friend. He has been playing it since such a young age so definitely he will be an expert of that sport. He took a lot of time to get the ball in control, he took a lot of time to shoot with power, he took a lot of time to dribble it perfectly, and you did all that sooner. But who is a better player? Can you ever expect to play international matches of Football?

I don't ask you to give the answer of this question it is so obvious. But just ask yourself that why this happened. This happened because you left the work for tomorrow and your friend did it that day. So learning something in childhood takes time, but when you keep on doing the same for very long then your performance betters by multiple times in future. You get a J curve in your performance while this can not happen with adults.

So, those successful people about whom we are talking were highly skilled since childhood. They always worked on their skills to make them better. They failed many times in childhood, but that was just for fun. So when they started doing it professionally they didn't fail because they knew what they are doing. If you have done something thousand times then will you fear to do it outside your school?

The same thing happened with all of them. They had done the similar things many times that later on they didn't fear that they could not do it after dropping out of the college.

Suppose if you are a very good debater so will you fear when you will go out of your college for competitions. You may lose but will you fear while speaking? Will you start fumbling? Will you start stammering? If you have done this in your school, college many times and you believe that you are good at it then you will not fear. Nervousness at the result time is different from fear while doing something. So they were not fearful of failure in work, but always the result rests in the hands of God.

They have started creating things with their skills when they were kids. They were not thinking that when they will get any job then they will do something with their skills. But they always had the desire to do something with their skills today. they took responsibility and did things. For them there was no tomorrow so whatever you want to do, you need to do it today. Here I have a few examples for you:

When Mark Zuckerburg was just a kid, he showed his interest in computers. His parent saw his interest and then get him a computer and every week his tutor came to him to teach him computer programming. His parents could easily afford it for their child. So the tutor started teaching him computer programming. Then he created a program called Zucknet for his family. Zucknet is composed of two words : Zuckerburgs and network. So it helped his father very much. He was dentist so now the coworker would not yell to call the next patient. At this time, he was very young, and this is not the end of his things.

Elon Musk was just nine years old when he read the computer guide which would come with all the computers of that time. He read that to get knowledge about computers but then he was so excited to do something, with that he created his own computer game. He then sold the game to a company for $500. He was just a kid but this thing could not stop him from doing anything. He read a lot, this was the result of that only. He read much more than any other person of his age.

Now I think that I should tell you something about Warren Buffet. You all may be knowing that he is such a great investor. But what I loved most about him is the fact that he started investing in the stock market at a very young age. He invested first time, when he was just 13 years old. Can you believe it that a 13 year old, invested in the stock market. And what I love even more is the fact that he faced a loss in that investment, but he kept on doing investing. He bought 3 stocks for $38. Then the price of the stock which he bought started going down. He became nervous, and it is obvious, since it was all he had. Then by luck the price came to $40. So he quickly sold all his stocks. Then after a few weeks only the price was up by $250. Technically, he didn't face any loss, but he felt that he had a loss by heart. So he learnt this thing and then invested by thinking long term, and today he is one of the best investors in the whole world.

I have many more examples but they are inside this book so keep on reading. I think that my point has been clear till now. They have always worked hard on skills and they gave time on this thing. They gave less time to stupid orthodox study. I used the word orthodox because we even don't know why we are studying, we are just following others, and they are also following others, and finally they are following us as others. This whole thing has been done since very long times, and now we even don't know why we are studying. We just go to get a degree, to get a job, and just it. We don't intend to learn anything. We should know why should we study and how much should we study? I have said that how much we should study depends on each individual and that varies from one person to other person. This point will be discussed in the end but till that time I hope that all of you would have already come to know that because that is being given in this whole book.The other point, why should we study and go to schools will also be cleared in the end.

Chapter 2: They Read A lot Of Books On Many topics

Well, I ask you that how many books have you read till now? And one very important point, textbooks and side books of any subject should be excluded from this. Now tell me what is your answer. If I ask you to exclude story books or novels, so now what is your answer? Well, I don't discourage you from reading story books or novels, they are extremely beneficial since they help in developing our vocabulary. But I mean others which develop our thinking. I mean biographies of great people, books related to your passion (on any subject or topic what you want to be, may be of a subject but of higher level, for which you will not get marks), encyclopedias. So what is your answer? If you have given your answer so now just search on the internet that how many hours does those people about whom we are talking read books?

They read books everyday. They read for hours, to gain knowledge. The books which they read were not only based on a single topic, but they were on varied topics. They read books out of curiosity and they didn't want to get a benefit from it. At the time of reading they didn't intend to get profit but later on, it was always used by them. They were very passionate readers. About this I would like to share a few stories with you, and I hope you understand what do I want to share.

Elon Musk was a keen reader from a very young age. Since childhood, he was having this passion for reading. Do you know how many books are there in the library in your school? Most probably you don't know, but he read all the books in the library. Can you believe it that he read all the books in the library. Then he requested the librarian to bring some more books so that he could read them. He loved reading books on various topics.

This can be seen in the companies he founded. Most of you may be knowing that he is the CEO of Tesla and Spacex, and may be about his contributions in SolarCity and OpenAI. But do you know that he started several other companies that I could not name all here. I have already told you that he developed a game which he sold to a company for $500. Then he created a website called Zip2, which was like a Map. Then he sold the website and then started another website called X.com which is used for receiving and giving payments. But a similar website was started near them which copied their all steps. So then both these companies merged together. The company was then named PayPal. Yes, this is the PayPal we use today. This was then sold to ebay.

Then he started his company Spacex because he could not get cheap rockets, so he wanted to reduce the cost of space travel by creating reusable rockets. He initiated this, and on the other side invested on Tesla because he could see future in that company. They were creating something which could change the world according to him so he invested there. Then Tesla was not doing very good so he even became the CEO of the company. Then he invested in SolarCity because again he saw the future there.

So you see on how many broad topics he is working today. So how is he doing this? He is doing this because he has knowledge in these things. He got that knowledge by reading books, and books, and books. So I hope that you understand the importance of reading books. But I want to share a small incident of a great personality in the following paragraph.

I think, that most of you may be knowing Bill Gates so I want to share one of his stories regarding reading books. Since childhood, he was also a book reader. He loved reading books. But he loved one more thing very much and that is operating computer. He was once denied the use of computers by his parents because his parents were worried that their child is going in wrong direction as he remained at the computer centre till late nights, as computers were very big and they could not be installed at homes. Then instead of crying in front of them he agreed. It was so simple for him. He then started reading books all the time.

You would have surely heard of parents scolding their children for not studying, and giving orders to study. But with Bill Gates it was totally opposite. He was very interested in reading books. Actually, he was so interested in them that he brought them to the dining table. He would even forget eating at that time so his parents denied him to read books at the dining table. He was a very passionate reader.

So do you see all of them were very passionate for reading books, or for everything. But just suppose if you also dropped out of school so the textbooks which you study or the knowledge which you get about the topics given there, would be ever installed in your mind. Do you understand what am I saying? So start reading books and knowing about different things.

Actually, the motive of this book is not to make you feel that you can't become successful if you drop out. But the motive of this book is to tell you the reason that how they became successful and how can you also become successful. If you can follow their steps then most probably you can also become successful. But remember I am saying to follow them, not copy them. I hope you understand it.

I think it should be clarified. By follow I mean that you should adopt the good things from them. You should adopt the habits given here in this whole book. But I don't mean to do exactly what they have done. They did what was good at that time. The time has changed and may be the step which was good at that time is not good at this time.

Bill Gates started a software company at the age of 20 and he became extremely successful. But if you do the same then will you become successful? Lets make the predictions. Software is of many types, broadly: System software and Application software. Microsoft mainly sold operating system software, Windows which comes under the first category. So you may have used Windows, so are you going to switch anyhow? If a new company comes with a new software so will you buy it from them? May be not, because you already have a good thing.

Even if software is good no one is going to buy it from you. But can you make something better? They have thousands of employees, huge amounts of funds and everything they need. Can you even get that much resources? At this time. Becoming a leader in that market is very difficult. But then how Microsoft grabbed the market?

Actually, Bill Gates and Paul Allen(his partner) saw the potential of computers and that everyone is going to manufacture computers. So they would need a great software for a great hardware. So they predicted the future of computers. There was no software companies giving really great software that was also easy to use. Therefore, they sold Windows and became so successful.

So following Bill Gates is to try to see the future and create what is lacking in the market. Try to make the lives of the people better as he did by creating a good machine easy to use. And copying

Bill gates means, without thinking anything drop out of college and create a software even if you don't know coding. So this is what I want to say about following these people.

Chapter 3: They Started While Studying And Then Dropped Out

This is very obvious and I think that all of you know that they had started working on their dream project in their college only. Some even used their college assets to start their project. Mark Zuckerburg hacked his college servers and he got photos of all the students. Then he started his website, FaceMash. This is like the basis and his training for Facebook. In this website, you were shown photos of two people and then you were asked to select one of them as hot and the other was not. This website gathered huge numbers of teenagers who used this website. He even used the servers of his college to keep it online. So due to heavy load the servers could not sustain to work as they did. Then college asked Mark to come and explain everything. And as he is doing now, after the Facebook scandal, he took the responsibility of everything and his college gave him another chance.

Well, the problem with FaceMash, even after getting so many users, was that some people started disliking it. They disliked it because they didn't get the hot tag again and again, so they started leaving. If this would have been continued then people would have been coming and coming and then could not have got the large user base as Facebook has got. They learned from there and then started this company.

All the drop out billionaires follow a similar path, Bill Gates with Paul Allen started his company in the college only. He used the college computers to create a software for the latest microcomputer Altair 8800. They created it together and then Paul Allen went to their office to show them this software. They liked the software and their concept very much. So then Microsoft started as a secondary company for them to create software. But soon after this company was sold due to its bad performance. At that Microsoft came out as an individual company. But when he was going to start all this he gave a leave application to the college but he returned years later, to receive his honorary degree from the college. But one very important thing, in Harvard University, you can take leave of any period and come back. So, this is very great thing.

Now one thing would have been clear in your mind that they didn't drop out to do something. They dropped to grow what they had. They were having great ideas that could change the world and they had started their own companies which were doing good, and which could grow very much in the future, but only if they worked on them seriously. They knew that they could make their companies very big. It is like that someone has told you the number of the lottery ticket which will win and you didn't buy it. They knew that even if they fail, they would be having experience and skill to get a good job. You need degree to get a job in the starting. But when you have done a job then you are asked for experience and skills. So they were having both these things.

It was like that they were in sky, they could fall anytime. They tried to stay there and they remained there. But if the worst would have been done to them then they could have fallen. But if you fall from sky, you will at least land on a big palm tree. You are there in a few seconds while others take years to reach at that place.

This is very clear that they didn't want to drop out at any time. They never wanted to drop out, but they were forced. No one from outside was forcing them but their situation was forcing them. I have told you earlier that they were working on something big, and which was expanding very rapidly. In the 2000s, you may be knowing how rapidly was the internet growing. It was growing many times each year. Its statistics from surveys told this. So if you were at their place could you leave the company which aimed at something which could change the whole world?

No, my answer to this question is no, and I hope that yours is also no. But if your answer is yes, then sorry to be rude, you are not capable to read this book. Just go and read some kindergarten story books. Well, I don't say this because you are not intelligent but because you are not of the mentality who are supposed to read this. And if you will study kindergarten story books then you could change your mentality. This is because the morals of the story could be easily understood by you. So this can help in developing the mentality to read this book.

So if we are capable enough of taking a right decision then how can they take a wrong decision at that place which could destroy their career and their family's future, and how could they leave the chance of helping millions or billions of people worldwide. So they took the hard decision to drop out, but not as many people think. They just gave an application of absence but it was different in case of Steve Jobs and it would be discussed in the later chapters, I expect it to be there if I don't forget to write it.

So they dropped because they were forced by the situation, the company, the feeling to help everyone and their desire to change the world for better. They were not happy while taking such a decision. They tried their best not to drop out. Yes, they tried not to drop out. They tried to work and study at the same time, but the work was intense and study required lectures which killed time. But you can understand how difficult it is. If you are a student then studies may be very difficult for you and if you are someone working in an office then you may be knowing that how difficult is your life. You don't have time to relax, you don't have time for your family, and you even don't have time for yourself. But they tried to do both the things together. But the work of the company was increasing continuously as the company was growing. They could not even think of decreasing the company's growth so that they can complete their degree and then work more after graduating.

This thing was killed by the thinking of the competition. In which field they were working was extremely competitive at that time. So slowing means destroying the company and giving someone else the chance of changing the world. So could you do this, according to you?

This is very easy, obviously no one can take this chance, so they didn't. Then finally they dropped out. So you would have come to know that why they dropped out, and even they became successful. But this is not over. There are some more amazing points which will open your eyes, and you will know the reality of their success. This will remove the illusion of luck from your eyes, that they were lucky. Many people say that they got early success, but I totally deny this. And if you want to know why, then keep reading this book.

Chapter 4: They Had A Clear Path Of Future

I have told you many things that they were working, they were earning, since childhood they read a lot of books, but can this alone result in that much success which they achieved? Well, being true, this may not be possible because this is too big. Their success is too big that everyone can't manage to get it. So why did they achieved this success even after dropping out. I can give a one line answer but before that I would like to discuss about the life of people who spend all the time in studying the books of college. Then it would be easier for you to understand that why did these entrepreneurs became that much successful.

Well, if you are student then it would be very easy for you to understand. If I ask you that what does your school or college want from you then what would be your short answer? You may thinking of saying to study properly, or to get knowledge or to become successful in life. But later on, you will say to get marks. They just want you to get good marks so that when you leave others can come because of the higher percentage of students. I exclude certain colleges from this because they don't do this, or they don't need to do this. I don't think that this is the motive in Oxford University or Havard university and few more. They have shown their potential to everyone already so they don't want their students to get good marks only, but they want to make their children capable and successful in life. This is the reason that Harvard gives its students any long leave if they want.

So if someone is studying just to get marks then what is his mentality? He just want to learn things until exams are not completed. Then he don't want to read that thing again. He just wishes to get good marks and the best part is that colleges encourage this. They want more marks. So a good child will focus on studies all the time (thinking that he will not cheat). So if he will study all the time then where is future planning? And if you think outside of college, or of future then they tag such students as bad students. Most people don't want such tags so they will try to be good, and will be nothing.

Are you totally dependent on getting job from the college because of your good marks? So if you get a job at a very good company, and at the age of 45, you become the CEO. So can you expect to get the success which these drop outs got?

No, you can never expect this. Even the highest paid CEOs didn't achieve this much success, if they are not the founding members of the company. Sundar Pichai is the CEO of Google and Alphabet. He is a billionaire, but nowhere near the founders.

Do you know the reason that you can't get that success? The reason is that you aim for small. The day you were dependent on getting job, you set an extremely small target. You achieved that target, but your success is small because your target was small. Your knowledge, skill and everything is nothing this time. If you aim for small then success can't be big because efforts reduce when you achieve targets.

Set your targets ridiculously high, so that you fail higher than other' success. This is something that they have in mind, even today. If this wasn't the case Elon musk would not have been working more than hundred hours each week on Tesla and SpaceX. He has set ridiculous goals and now want to achieve them.

You don't know that which kind of job you are going to get, you don't know in which company you are going to be part of, you don't know if that company is good for you or not, then how can you prepare yourself for the job which you will get at that company? What would you do if you don't get a job? What will you do if you get a job at very small pay? What will you do if the company fires you soon after? And many more questions are there in my mind, but do you know the answer of any of these?

No, you don't know. You didn't know what are you going to do in future. You knew nothing about your future. It is because you were not doing what you want but you were doing what others wanted you to do. If you will not work to complete your dreams, then others will make you work to complete their dreams. You want to get a good life, a good career but you were giving all your efforts on studying to get good marks. Can those good marks help you when a company fires you? Can those good marks help you when you don't get a promotion for decades? Can those marks help you when you need money to pay the fees of your kids?

No, good marks are very bad. Well, I want to tell you a story about a boy named Harry, but not Potter, and think of him to be you and think what would you do at all the places.

Harry was a boy who got good marks in school then his parents wanted him to do graduation. He chose 3 subjects to do graduation. His college starts and he was really good in studies. He got the first rank in 2 subjects but he got 15th rank in the third subject. The reason was that he didn't like the third subject much. He wanted to get a career in the first subject that is Physics, but the third subject was Maths. His college saw his potential so his teachers advised him to focus more on the third subject, his parents advised the same. So then be followed the advice and worked more on the third subject.

The next results came and he was first in 2 subjects and fifth in the third. Everyone was happy for him.

In the same college he had friends. Those friends were good in studies but not like him. One of his friends was Sam, he got 7th rank in the first subject and 19th and 29th in the other two. He was the weakest in the group of intelligents. He also wanted to achieve a career in Physics, but he never paid much attention to the other two.

Then time went on, the final exams had just finished and now its time for the results. Harry got the first position in all the subjects. His friend Sam got third position in the first subject, and has marginally passed in the other two. Then they both applied for a job, they both went for interview and from both of them several questions were asked. They both did well according to them. Then the result was that Sam was selected and Harry rejected. It was just a week since the results, and no one knew that how it all happened.

Then Harry went for post graduation but at that time he was extremely confused that which subject he should take. He could only take one subject so he was confused between Physics and Maths. He wanted to have a career in Physics, but he thought that by doing this all his hardwork in Maths would go vain. Then finally, he decided to take up Physics because he could get good marks in it, as he thought. Then after the first exams, he could not perform well there. He thought that all his answers were correct. So he went to his teachers to ask for this. They told him that his answers may be correct but they were for the other subjects which he had studied and paid a lot of attention. He had started to think in that subject so his answers were of those subjects. His matter was not of the subject he is studying.

For example, let's suppose we are studying Physics. Why should we wear seat belts? The answer is so that if we stop the car suddenly we don't hit ourselves forward due to momentum. But if you wrote so that we would not be fined by the traffic police. It can also be correct but in other aspects.

Now he thought that not only his all hard work has gone vain but also that has spoiled his skills in his favourite subject. Now he even came to know that why Sam was selected for the job. Actually, Sam studied more only one subject that, is Physics. So whatever he knew was of Physics. He lived in Physics world, he thought in Physics. After conversation with Sam, he came to know that he didn't study only the syllabus, but he also studied other things than the syllabus. He studied that because he loved Physics. Other things does not matter to him much.

The company wanted someone good in Physics, so they didn't care about other subjects knowledge. Therefore, he was selected. Why he didn't secure first position in Physics? Because he studying other than the syllabus that might be useless in college but very useful outside school. Then Harry understood this and then paid attention to the parts of Physics which he loved. He didn't pay much attention to the other parts. Then he was selected by an aircraft company, which didn't care about his knowledge in other subjects. Actually, he used his knowledge of other subjects in his job later on, but only sometimes. Having knowledge on other matters is not bad but problem arises when you pay more time than needed.

You know that some knowledge is more useful for you, so give more time to that, pay more attention. But what Harry did was that he gave more time to the subject which was less useful to him. He didn't maintain a balance. Sam didn't study other subjects, so when when he needed knowledge of Maths or Chemistry he checked it on the internet, or asked other people. Studying them in the college he had a little overview of the subjects.

And being true, the overview which remains with us after after one or two years of studying a subject is almost same for everyone. It does not matter whether you are a topper or not.

He got that knowledge only that much as needed by him, not more. And it was enough for a good career. He paid that much attention which was needed, not more.

I don't say 'Don't study other subjects', but I just mean that you should be focusing for knowledge of purpose only. It should be like giving your everything to that. Knowledge is infinite and if you think or anyone says, we should know everything, then that guy knows nothing. You can't know everything even if you live thousands of years. You have a small life so focus on what you love and what is useful.

Harry would also not have paid more time to Maths if someone was there to give them this knowledge or this story. When you focus on your weakness, you become average. But when you focus on your power you become the best in the whole world. I say spend time in the thing you are the best. You can leave the things in which you are bad if you want, but I say, try them for fun. Try them as timepass. You can definitely give them little, but with this approach you will not be stressed and don't care for the result. You are having fun and learning that thing too. That's it, the approach to learn what you don't like. You don't need to be the best in that.

So I hope you liked the story and came to know that why college is not always good. They want to get their good from us. So this may be enough for you to know that why these entrepreneurs are so successful. They didn't want to focus more on less important things. They were being taught what will be less useful to them in future. That could the part of the subject they loved. It may also have happened that they already knew that because of book reading.

They had a project on which they were working and which could change the whole world. Their project could grow very big one day they believed. They were not dependent on job, so they were not dependent on degree, so they were not dependent of college for a good career. They were not confused that this is good, or that is good. They were sure of what they will do. And finally they didn't want to give their time and energy on other things. They had clarity and self confidence.

This thing is taken very seriously by Mark Zuckerburg and Steve Jobs and others. This is the reason that they wear the same clothes everyday. They don't want to waste energy and time on choosing clothes, so they wore the same clothes everyday. It requires little energy and time, and they think of it to be useless. Then how can they waste so much energy in studying other stupid subjects which they needed less?

They were extremely focused on their goal and future. They were even ready to change if they were wrong previously. Mark Zuckerburg had Psychology as his main subject in college. But very soon after realizing his mistake he changes it to Computer Science. They knew the next steps to be taken by their companies and they knew the steps to be taken by them. Dropping out was a small step, if they needed to take even riskier step, they would not have stepped back. It is because they were extremely passionate and sure of the success of their company. It was only because the path of their life and company was so clear in their mind. They all were extremely visionary people.

Chapter 5: They Were Working For Very Long Hours, Even For Nothing

Yes, this is very correct statement that they were working for nothing. They didn't want to take rests or they missed weekends. They were never interested in holidays because they were doing what they loved. They were working for success, not for holidays. They knew that they were doing much more work than they needed to do in the college, but they kept on. They tried not to get such thoughts because these could make them weak.

Their passion and hard work was limitless but the other important thing is that they were not being paid for this. They were working in their own companies, but they were not giving themselves any salary. It does not mean that the company was not generating any meaningful revenue. They were even paying to their employees. The company was generating revenue, but according to them that was less and taking that at the time, would harm the company in the long run.

This was what they thought. They paid their employees because they needed them, but without salary they would go. According to them, paying themselves at such a critical time when company was growing, taking salary was stupid. The reason was that the growth of company requires assets, marketing and money, so instead of earning themselves they were utilizing money in these things.

They didn't want to reduce the speed of growth by their small greed of money. They wanted to invest all the earnings of the company back into the company. They were visionary so they were seeing that a little problem today can make a better tomorrow, not for them but for everyone. They could have done cheating with everyone by taking more money that they deserve, and being true no one could ask any question. But they didn't want quick success, but they wanted big success. So they even sacrificed what they deserved for the company.

If they would have asked this to their early employees then definitely they would have denied. All the employees wanted money, but no one was capable enough to see the potential of the company and work for free. Working for free is not stupidity, but they would have surely got better stock options later on. This shows us the thinking of the employees.

Well, basically this is the difference between an owner and their employees, this is the difference between a visionary and non visionary person and this is the difference between a successful and unsuccessful person. They all were working at the same place but why only a few people could see the potential of the company and not others? Why only few were not interested in salary and not others? Why only few tried to change the world and others just wanted to do job and earn money?

I don't want to say anything on it. This is the difference between them, this may be the difference between drop outs and graduates, and this may be the difference between them and us. Being true, graduated can't do this. Actually, graduates spend a lot of money on graduation as fees. Their parents have invested a lot of money in their education, and may be they have taken a loan to support their education. This is very common nowadays. Parents are used to take loans for education of their kids. They think that it is the best thing they are doing for their kids, but actually this thing makes them fearful and forces them not to take any risk.

Then they need to get a job as soon as possible. Then after getting a job they need to earn money. They need to get salary every month. They want to be independent and they want to show this by repaying the loan which their parents took for their education. Sometimes, in this haste to repay the loan and family pressure they chose a job so quickly that they regret later on.

Regret can be of many types. They may regret that their company is not good because they have fired him soon after appointment. This may seem no problem if you are a kid. You may be thinking that he can search a job at other place. But when the officials ask for working experience, and why they left then it is a problem. Even character certificate is a problem that time. So they may regret because of choosing a wrong a company.

The other regret may be that they were in so haste that they didn't checked other vacancies. Other companies which were better than the company in which they are working are far more better. They are even giving more salary, and good work place, and other benefits. So this may seem not a problem but this is regretful. It becomes more regretful when one of your friends get a job there and he praises the company all the time. It becomes even more regretful when he is your dumb friend.

This regret is also very dangerous. This regret is that you are not getting promotion in the company. You have been working their for last 5 years and they have not given significant promotion. Then you have not learnt anything there as they are orthodox people who don't want to innovate and change with the world. Then how can you get a new job? You have not learned anything new. You have forgot what you learnt in the college (Be practical and most of the things were crammed by you to get good marks). It is a problem to get new job and you are not getting promotion also. The other problem is that the company is not innovating and it is not changing with the world. This company may be destroyed any time. So what will you do?

These are some of the regrets of taking a wrong job in haste to repay a loan. But what I suggest to parents is that they send their children to a lower college instead of taking loans that make their children fearful of future that they can't take the correct decision. Loan is like a gun pointed on head, then you are asked to get money soon.

Such a person may get opportunity to work with those drop outs about whom we are talking. He will work there but his fear of repaying the loan can't allow him to deny for salary and ask for stock options and other benefits which people get when a company grows. Neither I know nor you know their capabilities, but even I am sure they can't because they are fearful. This fear has closed their eyes of wisdom, and it has opened the mouth for money.

Well, another problem is that they even can't work in a start up. This is because a start up can't pay them much salary and they want more money quickly. They would try to get a job in a big company. The first possibility is that they can't. Can a college graduate easily get a job in Apple, Microsoft, Amazon or Google? But even if they reach there, can they grow that much as they could with a start up?

They can grow more with a start up because it is small and when it will grow big then they will also be promoted and they will also grow. Growth of start up is rapid and a matured company can't match the growth of a good start up, or the growth which they had when they were start up. But a start up will definitely grow very fast if you chose the correct start up.

This is very important part, you need to chose it carefully. If your choice is right you will be successful, but if you are wrong then your life may be ruined. But the other thing may be that you make the start up successful. Yes, you may be capable and smart enough to tell them what is wrong and then correct that thing. You definitely need to become a key part of the start up. You should not depend on them that they will give you instructions but you can show leadership qualities there. What do you think how does CEO, CFO and other posts are filled in start ups when they grow?

They are created by seeing the capabilities of the members. So show your skills. But if you started the firm then you are not the one who is chosen but you are the one choosing. You can choose yourself also but at that time you need to analyse everyone carefully. You even need to choose someones else for the post where you want to be if he is better than you. But you will always remain an important part.

The people who take loan make their children weak. Their aim of making them stronger vanishes as they try to give them education by loan. Either they should be sure that they will repay the loan, and for repaying they are dependent on their children. Otherwise it is very dangerous. It is just like buying Lamborghini when you can't afford Maruti Suzuki.

Therefore, drop outs are fearless. They don't have any fear. Do you know that this is the reason that Steve Jobs dropped out. Now I'm going to tell you that why he dropped out. Actually, he was an adopted child. But his real mother asked his new parents to sign a contract that they will surely send him to college. Actually, new parents were also drop outs. But they agreed and signed the papers. Then Steve Jobs grew and when he was ready to go to college he gave a condition. The condition was that he will only go to Reed college. It was extremely expensive college but it was his wish. His wishes have changed the world many times so how could he fail before his parents. They agreed.

He went there but then he saw that he is not learning anything new or interesting there. His only interest was the Calligraphy class there, but he never admitted into one, officialy. He started to think that he is just ruining his father's money there. Then thinking this he dropped out. He does not want his father to take further steps as they could not pay the fees which increased his desire to drop out. He was in contact with his friend Steve Wozniak then they started Apple computers which is today also. But the time till that was very painful. He was even not able to get food properly. He went to the RadheKrishna temple to eat food and for that he walked almost 11 km.

He didn't want to be under load of the loan. If that would have happened then we could not have got Apple. So his thinking was right and not just for him but for everyone.

Now I have one fact for you to know. Even before graduating high school Mark Zuckerburg was offered a job in Microsoft. Can you believe it? At that time Microsoft was the top company in the whole world. But Mark Zuckerburg denied. His decision was correct, but if he would have been under the fear of not being able to repay the loan then he would not have founded Facebook, because the idea striked in his mind in the college. He was not forced by his parents, so he could take the correct decision. Well, I appreciate his decision but I appreciate the Microsoft employee who suggested his name. His choice was so good.

So now you would have seen the difference between education which is taken with or without loan. So this is basically for parents. Please don't load your kids with these loans. They are just going to be the reason of wrong decisions. So strengthen your kids don't put so much load on them. They are kids, not donkeys to put load on.

Working for free does not mean that you are stupid but it really means that you are extremely passionate for something, and when you are passionate for something then you do it for success, not for money. Money is needed but to become very much successful you need to have a strong interest in something because it can make you successful. When you don't get money from there then you start using your brain, how? When you use this thing then you surely become successful.

Chapter 6: They Were Self Learners

As I told you that they read a lot of books and they used their skills in creating things, but have you ever thought that what were they learning in schools, or colleges? They were being taught what others were also being taught. They were asked to study what they already knew. This happens when you study on something very much. Sometimes you even start feeling frustrated in class, because sometimes, you think that the teacher is wrong. When you ask any question the teacher could not give a good answer to it. This is because that topic is just another one for the teacher but for you it is much more than that. You want to know everything about it, you want to use it as soon as possible but the teacher is teaching you the alphabets of the topic. On the other hand, surely there would be things which you don't know but they are of the kind about which you don't want to study or you will not use in future. I know that we use everything we learn today but this is not the way. In the previous story of the two kids going to college showed us that if we focus more time on the things we use less then it will be useless in the future.

They even study about new things themselves but the difference between studying ourselves and at school is that we are not forced to learn everything written. We just try to get what we want and leave what we don't want. But at school we need to know everything. But many times, important things are easy but difficult things are useless. Yes, believe me. All the times, when we see great things they are not always difficult, they are easy with just a little creativity dropped.

So they were coming to college either to study what they have already studied or to study what they don't want to study because they can't use it. On the other hand, their habit of reading and using knowledge to create things and capacity of self learning was making them skilled and they were also happy.

Suppose you force a fish to stop swimming and climb a tree, so what would be the status of the fish. They had this kind of feeling in the schools or colleges. They were not doing much good to them by attending lectures in the college. They were doing good by meeting to teachers whom they admired. They were doing good by meeting with new people and kids. But on the basis of lectures and other things, they were not doing anyone any good.

Their time in the school was somewhere a kind of a wastage. They were wasting their time in the lectures, and in the exams. While if they were not there they would have been reading something new or creating something new which is their passion. They never desired just to study something and then study something else. They always desired to use their knowledge all the time. It is since childhood that they had this attitude.

Do you know that at teenage, Bill Gates started a company called Traf-O-data. According to Wikipedia, Traf-O-data was a business partnership between Bill Gates, Paul Allen and Paul Gilbert. The objective was just to read the raw data from roadway traffic counters and create reports for traffic engineers. And do you know that they were just high school students. Can you believe it that high school students were working with the government. No one asked them to do this. Even, no one really encouraged them to do this in the school. But they did it. They created the required software. This was not easy for them but their desire was firm to create their first company. They were not learning this in the school as a major subject. But they worked on the computer just because they loved it. They learnt it because their school installed one system in the school. Many students didn't pay attention to the device called computer, because it was not going to give them marks in the exams. This is the reason that Bill could get sufficient time with the system.

They had a teacher who could teach them little bit about this strange device which is called computer. But most of the things these kids learnt themselves. They did self learning. Then after that they created such exciting products. Then surely they were increasing their skills. Then do you think that they need someone to teach them?

Well, being true, journey of learning with a good teacher is just awesome. Suppose if you need to study with Nursery kids and everyday you need to sit there for 6 hours and finally you need to give exams of high school. What would be your situation at this time? They were facing the same situation because they needed to attend lectures that were for beginners, as their other mates were, and then they needed to compete with the giant companies which had thousands of employees, which were experts. Just tell me what will you do if you were sitting with the Nursery kids? Will you go to the class or leave that and study at your home? I would leave the school and study and I expect that you would also do the same. So what is wrong if they did the same?

They were just giving their hundred percent in order to get the results which they wanted. You only get results where you work. They knew and believed that they need to get more and do big things. So they just tried to do that as soon as possible. If you think that this is just for saying, and no one really knows in childhood that they are going to be very successful, then you are not alone. Many people say this, they say that a person just boasts when he says that he knew it in childhood. But being true, I also told everyone that I am going to be very successful in childhood. I am not very successful this time, but soon I will be. Just remember my name, Genius Mehra, and please pray for me that I become very successful very soon. You may be thinking that I am boasting or I am just an arrogant person. Then I am not going to give any explanation, you can think anything and you are not wrong. But please just keep praying for me. I need it. And I am hundred percent sure that if you will pray for me then no one can stop me from being very successful, very soon. I bet with you.

Chapter 7: College Was Fun, They Wanted Challenge

Well, as I told you that were not learning very significant in the college. But they needed to go there. It was stupid according to productivity. So what could they have been doing at that time? Well, I was not there, nor were you. So lets think together. Assume that you have studied for the very first time, a topic before the teacher. Your tuition teacher has taught you that topic several times before also. Then in the classroom you saw that the the teacher was teaching the starting only. Suppose

you have learnt tables till 20 and teacher is writing the 6th so what you would do? You will try to tell your friends the answers before the teacher has written them on the board. You would definitely try to show off to your friends. When the teacher will ask to learn then you are free. You are relaxed. You would be talking to your friends, may be disturbing them sometimes, playing games with those who don't want to learn in the school. So isn't it fun? Will you not be enjoying those moments? It will be amazing because you are the best at that place, you are the one enjoying, you are the one free.

If you liked this feeling then think how would they have felt in the classroom? They could remain there being the best, but they knew there are people who are better. So they wanted to be better, they wanted challenges. They knew they need to compete with the best people in their profession. So for that they tried new things everyday. I mean, they just did what they loved. They created new things and had fun. But now they were trying to make things which are really useful. By useful I mean useful to the public that they could give money for it. They wanted to help millions of people around the world. They wanted to grow in the whole world. They had this desire and it stopped them from being ordinary and do what others are doing. They didn't want to just study, get a job and then retire. They wanted to serve the whole world. So they used their skills in helping the whole world.

Did you remember how difficult was it to talk to people when there was no Facebook? I know that you were having mobile devices, but do you remember the cost? Facebook made it very instant and cheap for all of us to achieve.

Well, how are you reading this book? Is this an electronic version or paperback edition? If this is electronic version then where are you reading this? On smartphone, tablet or somewhere like this only. This is just a small feature of these gadgets, they can do much more. But do you know how all this started? When Apple introduced its first iPhone. The whole smartphone market was disrupted. Then people gave it their love, so others also wanted similar thing. Then there came competition to make it better and better and therefore, it is as it is today.

But how all this started? It all started after computers. If it had not became easy to use computers then could you have been using a smartphone, or could anyone invest money in smartphone?

So did you understand what I wanted to tell you? It could have been a reality because they tried. But what could have happened if they passed their college, and started doing job due to family pressure. Then could they leave their job. Actually, they would have been getting huge sums of money. They would not be having any problem of money and they would have been living a luxurious life. So they could not have done all this.

But really does those kids had this much desires from earliest? Well, yes, but no. They were doing this because they wanted to challenge themselves. Could I create something that much useful, could I become the best, could I do it now, and many more were their questions to them. They loved challenges since childhood.

There are many stories showing all this. You may be knowing of the rivalry between Bill Gates and Steve Jobs. Well, all the people know of this rivalry. They could do anything to win against the other person. Actually, this is the reason of so much development of the world and smartphone market. It was a great challenge to them to win because their rival was very strong. They knew how much capable was their rival and what could he do? They respected each other but there is no space for pity.

They worked all day, and all night. All the time they were trying to be the best. But why? Because it was now a challenge to grow at that time. It was extremely difficult to see a computer at every home. But they dreamt of this and completed their dream. They were running behind their this dream. Ans now every person has a small computer called smartphone.

It was not just their dream, but a challenge they gave to them. So they could do anything, but can't accept being defeated. So they did win in their competition with each other. They won against their competition with them. They won against everyone.

They could have been the best of small classroom, but they knew being a novice in a group of experts is better than being an expert among novices. Being with experts would force them to be better and will help them in becoming the best. They were with the market champs, and competing to win the whole market. So they tried and did it.

So have you given yourself any challenge such that you are trying to defeat yourself by achieving something big? If not, then is the best. Don't wait for the next year just challenge. Before reading any further just do challenge, then read ahead. After reading start your efforts to achieve. I will keep on posting more books to help you and motivate you. So read other books also because they all read a lot of books and you want to be one of them, didn't you? If you have challenged yourself then tell me.

Chapter 8: They Were Passionate To Make This World Better, Not Their Life Only

Many people nowadays are doing jobs at various places. I could even say that all the people are doing jobs except a few, who can be counted. May be you are one of them who do job. But lets think that why do people do a job? I don't know since I have not done it ever, but you might. So lets discuss. When we do a job, we get money every month regularly. We get a fixed amount of money every month. But being true, I don't get the same amount of money every month. Sometimes, I get more and sometimes, it is very less. So while doing job you are free of this variance. And while doing job, sometimes, you also get bonus. You just need to do a particular task and you will be paid. You don't need to take tension that whether the company is in profit or loss. You get paid regularly even if there is loss. You can even change the company when it is not giving you raises which you want. So these are some of the few benefits of doing job. I don't deny that there is security in job, but is job having only benefits? All the things have disadvantages also, but before talking about the disadvantages of job, lets talk of entrepreneurs or people not doing job.

We people don't get paid regularly. Being true, we even don't have this security that we will surely be paid. In the starting, there are times when we are not even paid every month. So what do we do at that time? Asking for help, using previous savings and other things. But when we get more money, then it is much more than expectations. We even get paid for about a year in a single month sometimes. If all the readers of this book recommend this book to 30 people and 15 buy it, then they do the same, and it goes on. Then I will be paid for about two years in about a month. And the best thing is that when our pay increases, our base pay also increases. This way our base keep increasing and therefore, sometimes, we think that our pay is almost nothing and we become sad. We compare it with the best time, and almost forget the earlier months. So this is our life.

Now comparing the two things, talking of money, then somewhere non-job people are at benefit. When we talk of work hours then there are no work hours. You can do work when you want. You can follow your mood. When we talk of holidays and leaves, then it is upto you. You can take any number of holidays, taking time out for work. Being true, all the days are holidays, you just work for a few hours. But sometimes, you need to work for 12 to 15 hours also. The starting is difficult but the future can be bright. So this is the comparison till now. When we talk of work happiness, then obviously, we people are happy because we don't have a boss shouting over our head. But if this the truth then why do most of the people do jobs? This may be a question in your mind. So lets give the answer.

When you have a job you are sure of getting a minimum pay each month. The maximum bonus would not be so much as there in the previous situation. So for security of monthly pay, people are doing job. But don't you think that their bosses can fire them? I don't mean for no reason, but can't they?

We are not talking of disadvantages of job, but why didn't those billionaires did a job for lifetime? But before that, do you know that Mark Zuckerburg got a job offer from Microsoft and AOL, even before graduating from High School. I told you this before. So why didn't he do that job? At that time, Microsoft was one of the top companies, as it is even today also. Well, Mark said that he never wanted to do a job. So what's the problem with a job to all those people?

Well, most of the billionaires have done job at least once but they never tried to settle in that. They aimed big and therefore, left the jobs.

I told you that they wanted to change the world for better. Suppose they did any job then could they get this chance? I don't say that you can't help in changing the world while doing a job. But somewhere you do have limitations work in a job and most of the people think that why do extra work than they are being paid? But while doing job they are bound. Every company has different laws and rules. They may be satisfied with few but not with other.

You may be knowing of the failure of Yahoo. Do you know that when Larry Page and Sergey Brin created the Google algorithm and full concept they went to Yahoo so that they can buy the algorithm, but they denied. Actually, Yahoo was making money by display ads. So they wanted the user to be on their website as long as possible. With the Google algorithm, people would find what they wanted soon, so they would leave Yahoo.com and go to the other website. So they took this step. Don't you think that out of many experts there, some may have seen the potential of Google algorithm and advised them to buy it? There is a 99% chance of this but the top executives didn't like the idea. So the lower employees were bound. This is a disadvantage of job when you don't want to just earn money. It is even bad for those who want money, because now we are seeing the position of Yahoo, so think of the position of employees. Therefore, all of these billionaire entrepreneurs wanted to change the world in their way and independent of others load on them.

A job could have given them money and a luxurious life, but they wanted more. They wanted to get satisfied with their life by helping as many people as they can. They have served millions of people worldwide by their awesome products. You may be knowing that billions of people use Facebook, billions of people use Google, hundreds of million iPhones are bought every year, almost all the household PCs have Windows. So this could have happened if they did job in a company with money minded top executives.

iPhone is the most important product of Apple. It came after the iPod. But the creator of iPod first gave the idea to other companies who could not see its potential and who didn't want to do investment in a product which has never been introduced before. But Steve did it, and after they got the idea of the iPhone which changed everything.

Do you know that these people never wished of luxury. Even now you may be knowing that Warren Buffet live in the same home as he lived years ago. Mark Zuckerburg is not having so expensive cars as he can, but even you can buy cars which he has, Steve Jobs was a billionaire but wore the same clothes everyday, Bill Gates could have bought anything but he donated so much of his money that now he is not the richest man on the planet. So they didn't want to just benefit them but wanted to serve the society and develop it. Money was just what they got for their hard work. But I will not deny that they wanted money. They wanted money but not to use it. They wanted it as a form of power. They wanted to be powerful, but not greedy or cruel. They wanted power to help others.

Chapter 9 : They Saw That Something Is Growing Very Rapidly, So They Didn't Want To Lose The Chance

Many time people say that dropping out was a wrong decision. It is because it was their luck which saved and they could have failed also. They could do what they did a few years after graduation and then they would be secured also. This is a point which is raised many times. But reading the this sub title you would have come to know that why was it needed to be done at that time only. Their success secret lies in their choices. They chose a field which was not very big. Being true, it was not very big but they saw the potential. They saw that they could become very big. So they started working behind their dream. They saw that this thing is extremely useful and after a few modifications it could change the world. So they did it.

Bill Gates saw that computers are very powerful. They could be of great help to all the people. But there was a problem with computers, that they are very difficult to use. For simple things you need to do a lot of coding and it was the reason that it was not being used at large scale. So he created an operating system which made using computers extremely easy for everyone. The market of computers was not very big at that time but it was compounding. Market was small so thinking of running a successful company which just created software was out of thinking. But he did it. He saw that computers are growing and he could grow the market much more than before by his software, so he dropped out. So few people say that he could do this later on also. But I don't think so. Do you think that he was the only smart person in the whole world? Others could also get that idea and if that happened Microsoft could not have grown that much. At that time, Microsoft was almost the only big software company. It was the reason that he won. But do you think that if now two undergraduates start a software company they could compete with Microsoft. No, definitely no. There are many reasons for this. First, they could not create a product as good as Windows, but if some how they did, how can they do marketing to tell people all over the world. How can they influence manufacturers to pre-install their OS in their products. From where will they get other applications for their software. Now users want much more than before. So it would be extremely difficult. There is a time for something and this is not a time to bet on an OS. The reason is that the world has good OS. People don't buy good products, they like problem solving products.

When Steve Jobs saw that his company is declining and to strengthen the company needs to launch a new product. So he introduced the smartphone. He saw the growing potential of smart phones, so he launched this device. He invested a lot of money and a lot of time. If it was a failure, Apple would have destroyed that time. But it survived, and now it is one of the most biggest companies in the world. But if he had delayed that then Android would have captured the whole market. Android now is the most popular mobile operating system in the world, but at that time Apple captured millions of users who don't want to switch and it is growing.

Well, when Mark dropped out he saw the potential of internet. He saw that this is something that can change everything. So he saw this growth and saw the problem which people face while interacting with each other so he connected these two things. Then came the website, Facebook. If he would not have worked on it then other people would have worked on other social networking capturing the whole market. Then Facebook would not have grown this much as it had done. Well, being true, Facebook was not the first social networking website. So then delaying much was a very bad idea.

If even after this much explanation you have not understood the value of time in life, then I have more very simple example. You may be knowing of YouTube. It is an online video streaming platform where people make a lot of money. Top YouTubers earn millions. If you knew this in 2010, then would not you have also made different videos on the app? If I started it that time then I would have been a millionaire this time, but I am not. I could not see its future as many other people. But a few people could. This is the case in other fields also. The few who can see the future become the most successful. But starting now is very difficult if you are not having a huge following behind you. You are not going to get views, rank and those millions now. Why? Just because of time. If they would have delayed then their situation would have been same as yours and mine. Now I think you have understood properly the value of time in our life.

If you have not understood then I have a great example. You may be knowing of Elon Musk. Well, he is working on reusable rockets and electric cars. Being true, his creations are making money, but not as much as they should. Because it is not a very big problem till now. But when fossil fuels will vanish then he will make a lot of money which you can't even imagine. He may become the richest person on Earth. Well, our actions towards Earth are also not great. So if we kept on doing it and earth became not able to be lived in, then we need to shift to other planet. At that time, his company SpaceX will make money. But this time, we don't want a shift so today it is not making a lot of money. But future is for him. He is working on things which are not the problem of the world, but which will become the problem of the world in future. His actions show immense farsightedness. He saw the problems of the future and he is working in their solutions from today. This is just awesome to see. You also do the same if you give your time to this. You need to give time to analyse the future. You may be wrong but after time you may make better decisions.

Chapter 10: They Had Great Partners

This is very true that they needed great partners. They needed great partners as catalysts to increase the rate of their growth. They needed loyal partners. Their partners needed to be skilled also. They needed to have mutual understanding in between them. So they all got them. If they would not have got those partners, then may be they would not have been as successful as they are today. But do you also have great partners with all the qualities listed above. If yes, then wow and if not, try to find out. They supported these drop outs at every situation to find the path of success. So lets think could they have got success without their partners? May be but may be not. So lets discuss it here only, because neither me nor you is a fortune teller.

Well, lets take different cases, starting with Bill Gates. I am starting with Bill gates because he is my inspiration and may be in future I will be an inspiration to someone. So what happened with him was that he always loved computers since the time a computer was installed in his school. He did many things. When he went to college, he studied Maths and computers there. Then MITS launched Altair 8800. It was a computer but it needed programming languages. it was of another technology at that time. Bill read the magazine but he was confused what to do. Then Paul Allen came to him. He influenced him to create the software together. So he and Bill together started to work and then they created it. Then it was Paul to go to the office of MITS. Their concept and software was liked by them. Paul could have deceived Bill but he didn't. He was loyal to Bill Gates. Then at every point, he was to help Bill. He was the one to influence Bill to drop out of the college. Then he took the decision and then he became so successful. It was he who brought the turning point in the life of Bill Gates and made him so successful.

When we talk of Steve Jobs then his story is also not very different. When he dropped out of his college, he used to go there for a few months. Then he went a spiritual tour to Kaichidham in India, then he started his company Apple. Actually, after coming from India he met his friend Steve Wozniak. His friend has always been a lover of technology and he always created different technological equipment. This time he created a keyboard and monitor. This was a revolution in the computer industry. Then Steve wanted to sell this gadget. They introduced Apple I but it was a failure. They could not sell millions of pieces as Jobs wanted. But then he used his mind and he gave a different shape to computer. He joined the screen with keyboard. At that time, mouse was not invented. So then he introduced his new product Apple II. They didn't change the technology but the way to present it. It was an instant success and both the Steves became very popular and rich. Then Apple kept on growing until Steve Jobs exited from the company. But we will not talk of that this time. We see that how much his success was influenced by his friend Steve Wozniak.

Mark Zuckerburg also started his website Facebook with his four colleagues. He also needed team. The most popular search engine was also founded by two people together, Larry Page and Sergey Brin.

You may be knowing of Indian billionaire brothers, Mukesh Ambani and Anil Ambani. Both had almost the same wealth a few years ago but not the net worth of Anil Ambani is not even 1/50th of Mukesh Ambani. Mukesh Ambani was sent to Stanford University but he thought that he was wasting his time there, so he went back to his father and worked with him in his company. While Anil studied in Wharton School in Pennyslavia. But he could even sustain his wealth. His money kept on decreasing and Mukesh kept on growing. He is on the verge of bankruptcy but Mukesh Ambani is the pride of India. But why? Because Mukesh Ambani invested long term in building his team to support him, giving good training to his children who are now supporting him. While Anil was just enjoying with all the money he had.

So now I advise you to also try making good friends. But not only to hang out but to give and take help also. So that you can grow together. Such relations become good in future many times. So now you would also be wanting to get a good team for yourself. But how can you do it? Well, I also don't know much so lets discuss.

If I want to grow with someone then I will try to know that who is having capabilities. So this is one of the qualities. After that you should see their passion to grow. Many people with extreme capabilities are not having any ambitions. So they should have a passion. Then they should have good attitude. They should not ditch you in any case. They should not be a bacteria to you. They should increase your speed but not slow you. Many people with wrong attitude do it. They keep on assuring you but don't take any actions to make your dream a reality. Just keep distance with such people even if they are extremely capable and ambitious. So I think you might have a rough idea of the qualities which your partner should have. But it is really difficult to find these people. But remember to get them you should also have the same qualities in you also. You also need to become a great partner to someone else if you want to grow extremely big in future. You need to make others also like you. So I hope now you can find good people for your team.

Now I expect that you may have got that why they became so successful even after dropping out of college. But till now many questions would have arose in your mind. So now its time to answer all your questions without wasting any time. I will try to answer all the questions but if I may leave any then please tell me in the reviews so that I can answer that in new book. You can even follow me on Instagram and Twitter on @geniusmehra. But now its time to answer your questions.

Question 1: Did They Get Early Success In Their Life?

Well, many people think they did get early success in their life. I don't think that it is true. This is totally a myth and a very popular myth. This is said to young children and they think that these successful people were just lucky and this often slows down their efforts to be super successful, but this is totally not the case. But how can this be wrong? We all saw they got success at such a young age? You may be thinking this but I have given the answer in one of the lines of above. Before answering your question I want to ask a few questions if you think that they got early success. Have you ever read whole biography of any such person? I don't mean a short 15 minute video on the internet or a short article about them. Do you know when they started their struggle to success? Do you know how much did they work at those early days? If you don't know these answers then you don't have the right to say anything to those people about their success. I ask you to read their biographies then you would not say that they got early success in their life. But if you want to get it in short then keep reading.

I want to give you two cases which would help you in understanding whether they got early success or not. John and his father, Ben, together started to learn a new hobby of painting. John was 5 years old and Ben was 28 years old. They both didn't know anything about painting. So they thought of hiring a teacher who would teach them this art. When the teacher came on the first day she saw that both of them were so stupid in this thing. But she was extremely passionate to teach them (since she was getting paid very heavily by Ben). So she taught them and then took a little test every month. They worked very hard. After 5 months, Ben became an Ok painter. He was not so good and also not bad. But John could not learn at the pace of his father. But he kept on working hard. After 15 months, they left the teacher and worked themselves. They worked for fun only because they were quite good painters now. None of them wanted to make it more than their hobby.

In this story, who among them got early success? Well, if you say John then you are wrong and if you said Ben then you are right. He got early success because he learnt this at a little faster pace than John. As we can see in the story. He learnt this earlier than John, so he got early success. This is what this term says.

But, who among them got success at young age? This is definitely John. At the age of 28, Ben knew nothing of painting, but John is a good painter at a young age of around 11 or 12. so he got success at young age.

Actually, all those drop outs have not got early success. They have got success at young age. There is a difference between these two things. Actually, getting early success means that when you start something then it becomes very popular very immediately and you become successful because of that. But they worked for months on a thing and then they became successful. They needed to leave almost everything while working. They worked for hours and were not paid that much at that time. But they kept on working on their dreams and projects.

In that attempt they failed many times but they got up again as soon as possible. Have you also tried doing something different like a start up? Well, most of the people say no to this question because they could never gather this much courage to invest some money on their ideas. And if they invest a little money and they face loss, they leave it. They don't give a second attempt. They themselves don't believe in their ideas. They ask for opinion to people. If they say yes, then they may try but if they deny they start doing doubt on their ideas. But do you know in either case, whether the public advises you to do it or not, you have a loss. Do you know why? Suppose you have any idea. Lets assume that Google is not created, or any other search engine and you are in 1990's. You got the concept of Google. You asked for advice. What could be the advice of people? Will they say yes, you should do? They will never say yes. In 1990's, people used internet less. So if you would try this search engine start up, it will be a loss to you according to your family and friends. Why, because if it was profitable anyone else would have tried it. Internet was so slow so how could you make good money with it. Advertisers at that time were not investing too much money in online marketing at that time. People didn't have proper knowledge of computers and internet.

So did you see that even the idea of Google would have been denied by your family and friends, so just leave any other small idea.

But there is one kind of loss left. What if they said yes? Suppose after 5 to 6 years after the introduction of Google you asked your family, then they may say yes, because Google was earning good money. Advertisers were also investing money online. So your family may think that you may also earn good money. But was that really a good option. Actually, there are tens of search engines but you just don't know them. The reason is that Google has become so popular. So you may have got a loss here also if you applied the same concept of Google. So do you see the effect of a few years. Suppose you had the idea of creating such a search engine and you had resources also. But you didn't want to drop out of college because you are topper in college. You would launch the search engine after graduation. So do you understand what can this time cost you. Sometimes, playing safe is the most dangerous step. You need to take risks, but calculated risks. Suppose if you had failed in that fight against Google. So are you going to die of hunger? Definitely, no, because if you competed a little Google may have seen your capability and you can do merge with them or get a job there. So is getting a job there small for you? Being true, there is no loss for you if you did it.

Actually, I don't discourage you from taking suggestions but actually most of the times it's useless. It is because they just want to see you secure rather than successful. But it is just their love for you. Don't take it in a negative way. May be if you were in their place you would do the same to them.

But do you know there is a way to know 100% that you will become successful in a field or not. Do you want to know that way? If no, then good but if yes, then sorry because you need to wait for my next book in which I will tell this. I can't write about all the topics in one book only. But forget that and read the other question and their answers.

Question 2: How Not Having A Degree Helped Them?

Has the author gone made? If you think this after reading this then it is normal. But after reading completely you will also become mad like the author. You may think like this crazy author. But now without wandering around other topics lets talk about this. But I am not a billionaire, so I also don't know so lets discuss together.

Well, suppose you have graduated from a college, prestigious or not does not matter. So you have graduated then now you thought of starting a new start up. You created a start up of messaging app, like Whatsapp. Suppose you were the founder of this app at the same time. So you worked very hard and invested money in its creation. Then you launched this on Apple Store. You could launch it on Android also but I am telling what they did. Then you wanted to get a lot of customers instantly, but what happened you could not get those users instantly. But you worked hard on it even though, but it could not grow even after months. Then what would you do now? May be you are thinking that it is a stupid idea on which you invested so much time and money. So now you may leave it and try to get a job since you are graduated. Then probably you will get a job, low or high depends on you. So now your job life will start and your entrepreneurial life ended. But do you know what happened with Jan Koum and Brian Acton (founders of Whatsapp)? Actually, they believed on the product very much and supported each other when one was losing hope. So they remained there after you also. Then Apple introduced a new feature of notifications in which the user gets notification from the apps installed in their system. So this helped in growing and we all know where it stands today.

So even if you had got the idea of Whatsapp you would have failed due to a college degree. But now lets suppose you didn't have a college degree at that time. You could not get a job(you would think this only). You needed to be with this app only, because it is the only thing with you. So after the change of Apple you would have become so successful.

So do you understand how not having a degree helped them so much. Actually, they wanted to change the world and make it a better place. But what if they face difficulty in achieving their dream? Facing difficulty is so common in this dream. So they may at last end up making their life only good. So not having a degree forced them to be successful and make this world better. If they could not become successful then they may have got a good job but how can they be sure? They didn't know that they have become so capable. As it is said for elephant that in childhood an elephant is tied with ropes which he could not break. So even in adulthood he does not try because he thinks he can't. They became capable but they didn't know they have become capable of getting a job in a good company.

Well, I understand that the example of elephant was not a perfect one to be given here but I wanted to tell you the power of thinking. They were strong mentally and believed that they can, so they did. They did whatever they can and they believed that hard times are going to end up soon when they will become successful. I advice you to also believe this that hard times are going to end up soon and please keep working behind your big dream because it is not just yours, but it can help many other people. And I also advice you to advice your friends to read this book because it can help them very much. But don't give them your book because it will not help them much because you may be knowing that when you take a book from library how do you read that? But what difference is created after buying it. Just try to imagine and help your friends and family.

But now a very special thing here. Suppose you became very successful person in future. So now someone wants to make a film on your life. So will audience like your movie if everything was so easy and you got success, or when you failed many times, but stood up again and then tried again. Then at a moment invested your everything and if it does not work you would lose everything and then the atmosphere is so tensed and then you succeeded. Imagine which kind of a story do you want? I want the difficult one and I feel this is the sort of story of Elon Musk. I have done many things and I believe that any time my luck may change and I may become successful. May be the book you are reading will make me successful. It may become the most popular book like Harry Potter. And finally, why this became so successful is that you recommended this to your friends and they to their friends and this kept on. I have hopes all the time. But now lets leave it and come back to the topic.

Actually, I don't deny that education is important in our life but I say that it is not that much important in the way as it is considered. Actually, now education has become just getting a degree and then job, especially in Asia. We are not asked to do something to change this whole world. Actually trying something is considered foolish. So do we really need to go to schools and till which level? Actually this is the next question and it will be answered there only. So just keep reading if you are liking this book. I have put a lot of effort on the book so please enjoy it because your enjoyment is my reward.

Question 3: Should We Go To School Or College? If Yes, Then Till Which Level? Is The Level Same For Everyone?

Now we are going to answer all these questions. If this excited you then I advice you to take a break because you can't take a break after starting to read the next paragraph. So all your wish. If you are fully active and energized and have time then please keep reading. If not, then take rest and then read it but in one go. If you are going to take rest please give this book a positive review.

So, first of all why do we go to school, college? Now, please don't say to get education or because it is very important or something like that. I know that you all go to school for that but I mean why only at school? You can get that education at home also. Earlier people sent their kids far away with teachers with other students. But before that parents taught their kids themselves. And the children became educated. Actually, one problem today is that you need certificate of your education but if we leave it then you can get education at home. You may be knowing the story of Thomas Alva Edison. If not then the next paragraph is for that, and if you know then escape the next paragraph.

Once Edison came home from his school. He was very worried. When his mother saw him in this situation his mother asked him what has happened. So, he told his mother that his teacher has given him a letter and asked not to open the letter. She had ordered him to give the letter to his mother only. So he handed the letter to his mother. His mother read the letter. After reading the letter she started crying. Tears were falling like a waterfall from her eyes. Edison became more worried. So he asked his mother that what is written in the letter. So his mother smiled and told him that his teacher has written to her that she is a having a blessed child. He is a gifted child with extreme capabilities, and the school was not capable of him. So they could not teach him and his mother was advised to admit her in another school.

But she started teaching her son in home only. She was teaching him. She taught whatever was necessary. So this was the education of the greatest inventor till now, who is having more 1000 patents on his name. Then after many years his mother died. It was unbearable for him that the most important person in his life has died. Then one day he was seeing the old things of his mother and he kept on seeing because everything was having some memories. Then he got the letter which his teacher gave. He read and it was written that your child is mentally ill. He is not capable of coming to school so please keep him at home only. He became very emotional at that moment. The respect for his mother increased very much after this in his heart and mine too. His mother has turned a mentally ill child into the greatest inventor ever born till now.

Actually, I should not write this in book because it is not the topic but I would like to do a few comments about all this. His mother loved her son very much. But more than that she believed on her son. She believed that her son can do anything. Even though, the teacher and the school thought that he was mentally ill but she didn't. She ignored all that. But can you expect such things now. When a child gets less marks in exams or the class teacher says something negative about a child in the Parents Teachers Meeting then parents scold their children.

They just leave all their belief on their child because of that small negative opinion. But when next time they praise him then everything is OK. They even don't believe that the teacher may be wrong sometimes, and their child is right. There have been many instances that teachers do crimes on children, but how do they get promoted? Just because parents believe on teachers more than kids. Whenever a mistake is done then its students' mistake only, but the teacher is always correct. In short, here I only want to say if you are parent then you should believe on your child. Believe on him but not other's comments about him and his capabilities. They may be wrong so believe on yourself and your child.

Well, now coming back to the topic seriously. Did you see from this example that education is not only given in schools but we can get education at other places like home, by anyone. But we go to school only. For this lets define a school. A school is a place where many children come to study and there they are taught by a group of people who have specialized in a particular subject. They know other subjects also but are the best in the school in a particular subject. They devote their time to give their knowledge to children and for doing this they are paid so that they can work in a better way. For this, money is taken from students. Then for exchanging all this a management is required to work in between.

So this is a school. But why we go there? It is because now parents don't have time to teach their children. This is a reason of going to school. The other is that they are experts for a subject. One person can't be an expert of everything so our parents can't teach everything in the best way. So they spend money and send us to school.

Learning from an expert is a good thing. So somewhere going to school is a good thing and we should go to school. May be the subject in which we are interested , other parents don't have expertise. So we should go to school which offers the teaching of the skills or subjects which we like or we are interested. So now the next question is that how long should we go to school or college? Well, I don't mean that how many years are there till graduating from a college. But I mean how much is necessary. This time differs from person to person. So this is extremely complex to understand. And if you need more time to be in school, college then it is not bad. You may become very successful in future even though of this. So now we will talk of this question only and this may be long.

So, for this, we need to go to the purpose of the school. We go to school for learning new things. We go to school to get new skills and become better in those which we already have. School is meant to give direction to us that what we should do. We should know that what are our skills. So we should be there until we know what to do. We should come to know that what are we going to do later after passing from there. But how can we come to know that? We will come to know this when we will try new things. We should get an opportunity to try out new things so that we can see what are our skills. We don't mean to go to school just to study a few subjects like Maths, Science. We need to learn new skills also. We should also get a chance to use those skills in real life. We should get an opportunity to learn by trying. By this I don't mean doing practicals which have been going on since decades. Being true, those practicals could be easily crammed by students. And even teachers know this that students cram those practicals and they promote it. More than the practical, they give importance to the written proof of the practical, and give them marks. Students want more marks because they need a certificate only, and being true, those practical are not going to be used in that manner.

So I mean that we should give new opportunities to students. May be they fail, but its OK, because everyone fails. In the path of greatness you surely need to pass through failure. It is just a part of success. You become more likely to succeed each time you fail. So we need to develop this mentality that failing is not bad, but it is good, because after failing you know that you need to work hard.

Now I will write a story here related to the topic and I think that you may like the story, so lets start the story. Once upon a time, there were two boys Tony and Nick. Well, its not Tony Stark, don't take it that way. So they are studying in the same school. Tony and Nick are having almost the same capabilities(just believe it for now). They both are highly ambitious for their life. They want to get huge success. But they don't know how to get it or what they should do, but their parents have told them that school is going to make them successful. So they should get good marks. They knew this much only so they worked hard to get good marks, because they thought their marks are going to succeed them. They were taught different things at school like dancing, singing, painting. Tony was open to such activities but Nick confined him to studies because he thought that he was going to get success by studies. Then once a Robotics class was held there in the school. Tony attended it. He saw many new things and was interested very much. He searched on the internet as much as he could about this thing which was very new for him. He was having a small kit which he bought from those people who organized the class. He did very much research, learnt as much as he could. He tried different combinations. He even purchased new parts from his pocket money. Then after a few years when he was in 9th standard he left the school, because he wanted to form a small start up of robotics. His parents denied so he even followed them. But he started his dream project. Then he sold different robots to small organizations like schools (cleaning robots), government offices (remote control powerful robots). Then he became famous and his start up was growing very rapidly. So then he finally dropped out of school in High school. Then he never came to the school. But Nick kept on working hard on his studies. He got first position in all the classes. His parents were very proud of him also. Once a Career Counselling took place in the school. So they asked him that what he wanted to do in future. Then he started thinking but could not answer. When forced he was mumbling and then gave a very common answer, an engineer. When those people asked him why, then again he was just in another world. When they asked him in which field, he was almost about to cry but said Electrical engineering. They asked why this only, then he became very tensed to say anything. His parents were with him, so seeing his position they told those counsellers about his marks and grades.

Then those people told them that marks are different thing. He can't just study his whole life. He needs to use his knowledge which he had gathered, by studying in school. And for that he needs to choose a field. Then he will use some part of his knowledge more than the other parts. So choosing a profession is very important, and as soon we decide, it is better. But it should not be due to pressure from parents or anyone else. As soon as we will come to know this as better we can perform in our life. School gives the same education to everyone but everyone is not going to do the same thing. We need to study a few topics more seriously than the others and even our marks of all the subjects don't matter. Being true, marks of any subject don't matter because they just show how much answers you knew of that subject when the exam took place, but they don't show how much you know that subject noe, or how much you could study in that subject, or how much you can achieve in your life? But now it was too late for him to understand. Actually, he was comfortable with the school system of grading because he was good there. So he continued it and if I could not understand then how could his orthodox parents change. They were just happy with the grades and it went on. He continued securing his first position again and they forgot the couselling. But after completing his school he was confused. So his parents suggested him (or forced him) to do Civil Engineering. So he took admission there. He could get it because of his awesome grades.

But after the admission he was really disturbed. The matter was that he was very burdened. He didn't like anything he was taught. But he kept on taking classes. Then he just tried to prepare himself of exams, by using previous year question papers and cramming. This way he managed to get good grades here also. But after this, the challenge in front of him was to get a job. But again his grades helped him a lot. He got employed in a company because they were impressed by his grades (as it happened previously). Then when he started working he didn't like it. He never liked the work. He didn't like going to isolated places for construction. But he needed to go there. He was unhappy but his company was also very unhappy with him because he could not do his work properly. He was good in learning and giving exams but he was not good here. His seniors regularly scolded him a lot. But he could not say anything since he was junior. Then once they fired him. Everything for him was shattered at that moment. He was so tensed to decide what to do. When he called his parents they scolded him, and said to help him if he decides what to do. But as you know he does not know what to do. He was so worried and confused at that time, then his life was very difficult. So he took the easy step of dying. He died and all his worries. But he forgot that he is leaving his failure story which could have been a success story if he tried that time from the starting.

But what about Tony, he was just like Tony Stark. He became very rich because this department was growing. He did philanthropy also so he was very respected also. He had a great life even after leaving school. But how did this happen? I expect that you know why everything happened in their life.

Now I do expect that you have come to know everything that, is schooling, college important? If they didn't go to school, then tony could not have attended that Robotics and then we can't expect that he could have become what he is. Upto which level we should go to school? We should go to school, college as long as we don't know what to do. We can leave it when we get the direction of our future. Tony left the school in High school, but he became so successful. Just because he had something to put all his efforts. He chose a field which was growing at that point, so it was not saturated. If it had been a saturated field then he may not have been so successful, because he would be having big competitors, and a lot of people already having chosen their favourite producers. But it was raw and no one knew how big it could become. So he worked hard and made that field so big. While with Nick, he never got the direction. He even didn't know which study he should do after school. So he needed more time, or he should have thought over those counsellers. But he didn't because everything was smooth for them at that point. The illusion of smoothness is teh biggest reason of not trying. We think that if everything goes smoothly why worry.

He never tried to analyse the future. This is the reason that farsighted people become so successful in their life, because they not only analyse future problems but also future opportunities.

Does the level of education needed changes from person to person? Yes, that changes from person to person. The education Tony took was sufficient for him, which was very less as compared to Nick. But the education of Nick was not enough. He needed to study more so that he could find out what was his talent, but he failed to find out in his life.

So I hope that you have read the whole book and you liked this book. Well, I hope that I helped you a bit. If you think that I helped you then please recommend this book to your family, friend, relatives and everyone you could, so that they can also get a little benefit. Please also give a good rating and review about this book so that others can come to know that they should invest their precious time here and it is capable of that. All the best to you for your future and I hope that it will be very bright. But please don't forget to pray for me as I said I have done a bet.

Are You Successful Now?

This question may seem useless as you have just read a book and I expect you to be successful just because you have read the book. But believe me I don't mean that. I want to know that as you have read about all the successful guys and now you would be having clarity about success and mission of life.

Secondly, success is not about money and achievements. It is about thinking. How you see yourself? If you think of yourself as successful then now or then you will definitely be successful. As it is written in 'Rich dad Poor Dad' also that the rich dad always believed that he is rich even if he didn't have money. Money comes and go and you may not have money now but believe me you are rich and successful.

So, the same is the case with you. Start thinking of yourself as successful and you will be. Now, you have clarity of work and path, but you need confidence to really achieve success.

About The Author

Genius Mehra

Well, nothing much to tell about me. I am just an ordinary guy who wants to spread awareness about schooling, marks and education. I want to empower all the people and that can only be done by giving right education and knowledge to students. So, this is the reason I am working towards this campaign.

Thanks to social media by drop outs that we can stay connected. If you want to follow me then you can do it on Instagram and Twitter on @geniusmehra .

www.ingramcontent.com/pod-product-compliance
Lightning Source LLC
Chambersburg PA
CBHW080847170526

45158CB00009B/2661